Date 7/27/2008

Hidden Data and Metadata in Adobe PDF Files: Publication Risks and Countermeasures

Enterprise Applications Division
of the
Systems and Network Analysis Center (SNAC)
Information Assurance Directorate

National Security Agency
9800 Savage Rd. STE 6704
Ft. Meade, MD 20755-6704
(410) 854-6191 commercial
(410) 854-6510 facsimile

WHAT THIS DOCUMENT ADDRESSES

This paper describes procedures for sanitizing PDF documents for static publication. Sanitization for the purpose of this document means removing hidden data and dynamic content not intended for publication (for example, the username of the author or interim editing comments embedded in the file but not visible on any pages).

The types of PDF documents that are addressed by this document include those converted from source formats such as Microsoft Office, Adobe FrameMaker, and any other native application. PDF documents produced through unknown sources should also utilize these sanitization procedures for static output.

WHAT THIS DOCUMENT DOES NOT ADDRESS

This procedure does not apply to document types for which interactive content is intended for publication. Users who wish to employ interactive content in their PDF documents (such as fillable forms, 3D content, layers, form calculations, and embedded media) assume additional risk because these sanitization procedures do not permit the retention of these content types in the sanitized static output.

This paper does not address the issue of redaction, which is the complete removal of specific visible content within the source document (for example, the removal of an image or a name in the text of the document). That procedure is outlined at NSA's website: http://www.nsa.gov/ia (search for 'redaction').

SOURCES FOR FURTHER RESEARCH

The PDF format has been approved as an ISO standard, ISO32000. Adobe also makes the PDF reference available on their website: http://www.adobe.com/devnet/pdf/pdf_reference.html .

ACKNOWLEDGEMENTS

The National Security Agency would like to thank Adobe for their technical contributions to this paper.

THE FORMATTING OF THIS DOCUMENT

In order to better describe the contents of PDF files, examples of the binary contents are presented in some sections. To clearly identify these occurrences and make them easily distinguishable from the descriptive text, binary examples are presented in a blue textbox in the following form:

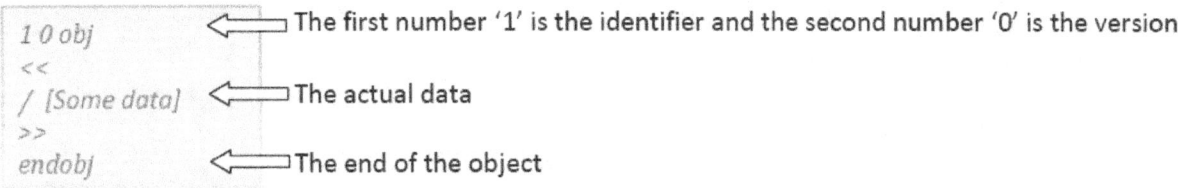

1 0 obj   The first number '1' is the identifier and the second number '0' is the version

<<

/ [Some data]   The actual data

>>

endobj   The end of the object

EXECUTIVE SUMMARY

The Portable Document Format (PDF) is pervasive and is used for publishing documents on the web, exchanging files between government entities and government contractors, and for interactive content such as forms and multimedia. Some of the reasons for its popularity include the wide availability of PDF authoring tools and freely available readers, cross-platform interoperability, and the ability to maintain the appearance of content across clients with varying hardware and software.

PDF has also been frequently used as a distribution format for files originally created in Microsoft Office because hidden data and metadata can be sanitized (or redacted) during the conversion process. Despite this common use of PDF documents, users who distribute these files often underestimate the possibility that they might contain hidden data or metadata. This document identifies the risks that can be associated with PDF documents and gives guidance that can help users reduce the unintentional release of sensitive information.

Table of Contents

Table of Figures

1 Introduction

The Portable Document Format (PDF) has become the de facto standard for sharing information electronically. The reasons for its success include the ability to retain the appearance of content across varying client types, a reduced threat of unintentional information leakage, and an increasing feature set that supports a broad range of user requirements. The increasing feature set and widespread use raise important questions about what types of hidden data these files may contain, how significant the risks are, and how the threat can be reduced.

When many people think of PDF files, they often think of Microsoft Office files that have been converted to this format. However, any application that can send output to a printer can interface with Acrobat's print driver to generate a PDF file. The potential for hidden data in these files varies significantly with the source application. In addition, new features such as forms may be created in Acrobat or using applications such as Adobe LiveCycle Designer that generate PDF output without requiring input from any external source documents. In those cases, additional hidden data may be transferred to the resulting PDF file.

There are many potential sources for data in a PDF document, but a user might not even know what the source was. As a result, if a user receives a PDF document and wishes to share it with a broader audience, it may be difficult to adequately determine whether sensitive data remains in the file unless they follow a careful sanitization procedure. New features and added functionality have also created additional opportunities for the unintentional introduction of sensitive data into PDF documents. This analysis defines the risks associated with PDF documents and outlines a procedure to reduce them.

2 Background

Adobe makes the PDF specification available on their website for developers in order to "foster the creation of an ecosystem around the PDF format".[1] The open availability of the specification enables a wide range of developers to create applications that can read and write PDF files. Variations (including errors) in specific implementations of these applications increase the complexity of evaluating the hidden data risk.

There are four major subsets for PDF, including PDF/X, PDF/A, PDF/E, and PDF/UA.[2] PDF/X is used mainly for graphics and printing. It includes enhanced color management and prohibits the use of active content that cannot be printed. PDF/A is used for archival purposes, and requires that major components such as fonts be embedded so that even if any dependent files are unavailable in the future, the file will still be displayed normally. PDF/E is intended for engineering with support for 3D content, rights management, and commenting features. Finally, PDF/UA files are designed for universal accessibility, so that disabled users and those who use assistive devices can effectively view the content. This analysis focuses on the basic PDF format and does not provide specific guidance for the subsets.

The PDF format has been used as a 'safe' format for mass distribution to a wide audience, such as when files are posted to a public website. Guidance to NSA/IAD customers for redaction encourages the use of the PDF format.[3] In addition to the reduced hidden data threat, PDF can be optimized for web viewing and site visitors only need to have the free Acrobat Reader installed in order to view the file. This benefit has further enhanced the adoption rate of PDF files for both government and commercial users.

The inherent complexity of formats such as PDF that can contain a wide variety of content types increases the likelihood that sensitive data may be unintentionally retained in the file. Understanding the inherent risks requires at least a basic understanding of the PDF format. Even though the format is 'open', understanding the structure and the associated risks is not a trivial task. The sixth edition of the PDF specification (Version 1.7) is 1310 pages. The content of a PDF file is typically compressed and may include a variety of different compression types, so extraction of individual components for analysis requires a combination of tools and techniques.

3 PDF Structure

PDF is a binary format that is based loosely on the PostScript language, and adds structure and navigation capabilities. The detailed implementation of PDF is moderately complex, and there are a wide range of developers who have created applications that generate or read PDF. With each different implementation, the possibility exists that the specifications were not followed exactly. For robustness, the Acrobat Viewer can reconstruct some portions of a file that are damaged or malformed. This feature enables the widest possible range of users to access PDF files that come from varying sources, but it also means that a file that does not conform to the specification may still open in the reader and potentially be difficult to identify as corrupt.

The contents of a PDF file may generally be read by a third party application and can be decomposed to examine the contents. One exception is where encryption has been applied. Encryption affects how the file may be read, but does not necessarily apply to the entire file. For instance, a document may contain metadata. Metadata is typically stored uncompressed in a file, so it appears in readable form in unencrypted documents. In encrypted documents, the metadata stream is typically also encrypted. However, if Crypt filters are used, the metadata stream may override the document encryption and force its contents to remain unencrypted (using an Identity crypt filter). For this reason, encryption may have varying levels of impact on the readability of the contents of a PDF file and apply only to limited sections.

The overall structure of PDF is fairly simple. There is a header, a body, a cross-reference table, and finally the trailer. An example is shown in Figure 1. The header contains the version number of the file. The body contains the objects that comprise the file such as text, images, and fonts. The body may also contain object streams, which contain a sequence of PDF objects. The cross-reference table and/or cross reference streams can be thought of as an indexes, as they provide the locations of objects in the body. Finally the trailer provides the location of the cross-reference table and potentially other items as well. Additional data may follow the trailer, such as update sections, which contain changes made to the file in an incremental update that overrides previous content in the file.

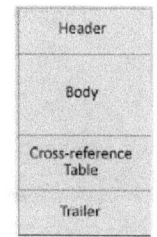

Figure 1 PDF Structure Overview

Header

A PDF file begins with the version number as the first entry in the header. The current version of Acrobat, version 8, can read files all the way back to version 1. The version appears in the first line of the file, and an example file that is version 1.5 would have an entry that appears in the form %PDF-1.5. For version 1.4 and later, this version entry may not be definitive, because an alternate version entry may exist in the catalog dictionary entry for 'Version'. A catalog dictionary is the root, or starting point, for accessing objects within a file. It describes how the hierarchy of the file is structured and includes information about how the file should be displayed in the reader. One of the scenarios where a difference may exist is when incremental updates have been added, and where the updates contain data that is a newer format than the base file.

While backward compatibility of new formats is not guaranteed, an older version of the readers and writers may still be able to read files created with newer versions of the file format. However, the newer features will simply be unavailable or hidden. The sanitization procedure that will be presented in this document recommends distributing the file in version 1.6 (Acrobat 7) because the active content that later versions facilitate will be removed during the regeneration process.

Body

The body contains objects of various types. Some of these types are simple, such as numbers, while others are complex. For example, subfiles with their own particular formats such as JPEG images, fonts, International Color Consortium (ICC) profiles, or PDF page descriptions are fairly complex. Objects may be stored as compressed streams, and content may be stored and compressed in a range of formats. Filters are used to describe how the data should be decoded. There are general filters and filters specifically intended for images. The general filters include FlateDecode, RunLengthDecode, LZWDecode, and ASCII85Decode, and ASCIIHexDecode. The image filters include DCTDecode, CCITTFaxDecode, JPXDecode, and JBIG2Decode. If encrypted data is contained in the file, the Crypt filter may also be present. The choice of format and level of compression vary with content type, but the range of options enables PDF files to be relatively small in relation to the size of the sum of their uncompressed parts. At the same time, this makes extracting and analyzing the contents trickier.

Each object begins with a header, in the form:

```
560 0 obj
<</Length 1005/Filter/FlateDecode>>stream
```

This example demonstrates the beginning of a FlateDecode stream that can be referenced as object 560, the first version (0) of this object, with length 1005. FlateDecode is one of the most frequently used types of compression for PDF version 1.2 and later files, and is similar to the ZIP compression algorithm.

When one of these filter types is encountered in a PDF file, extracting content from the streams for use in other applications is generally possible. For instance, the content where a DCTDecode filter has been used can be directly extracted and saved with a .jpg extension and should open properly. Other image types such as Bitmap are more difficult to extract, as they are generally in FlateDecode format, require decompression, and may be stored as separate color table and pixel representations.

The fonts may also be embedded with the file to maintain appearance across clients in case a viewer does not have access to any particular font that is used. Even for the same font family, the actual fonts retained within the file may differ between files. This occurs when the PDF conversion utility retains only the glyphs that are actually used within the file, and helps to maximize efficiency and minimize file size.

Metadata may be located anywhere in the file. Except in linearized files (those optimized for "fast web view"), objects in a PDF file can appear in any order. Furthermore, metadata streams can be attached at the file level or to any self-contained subassembly object in the file, such as a page. The file may contain a document information dictionary and/or a metadata stream. The document information dictionary (as shown in Figure 2) was used up until PDF 1.4. Starting with 1.4, an Extensible Metadata Platform (XMP) entry in XML format was introduced as a valid metadata storage mechanism.

```
1 0 obj
<<
/Creator (NameOfOriginalFile.doc - Microsoft Word)
/CreationDate (D:20071001144610Z)
/Title (NameOfOriginalFile.doc)
/Author (UserName)
/Producer (Acrobat PDFWriter 5.0 for Windows NT)
/ModDate (D:20071004091629-05'00')
>>
endobj
```

Figure 2 Document Information Dictionary

The newer XML metadata stream is shown in Figure 3. The XMP schemas define how the metadata will be stored, including what fields are available.

Following the XMP entry, a document information dictionary entry may also exist with much of the same data that was in the XML. For sanitization purposes, sensitive data must also be analyzed and removed from this additional stream.

Both the document information dictionary and the XMP entry offer significant potential hidden data threat avenues that should be addressed by removing this content from the PDF file before distribution.

Figure 3 XMP Data

Cross-Reference Table

The cross-reference table is the only component within the PDF file that has a fixed format. It contains references to the objects in the file by byte offset. The table contains entries in the following format:

nnnnnnnnnn ggggg [s] eol

n... is the 10 digit value of the byte offset of the referenced entry, g... is the 5 digit generation number (always 0 for an object in a new file, and this value gets updated when the file is updated and/or when contents are deleted), [s] identifies the status of the object (free or in use, using f or n), and eol signifying the end of the line character for the table entry.[4] An example of a cross-reference table is shown in Figure 4.

Figure 4 Cross-reference Table

Trailer

The trailer contains the trailer dictionary, which has references to:

- The cross-reference table (as well as the number of entries in the cross-reference table)
- Alternative cross-reference sections (if applicable)
- The catalog dictionary
- The encryption dictionary (if applicable, required if the document is encrypted)

- The document information dictionary (if applicable)

In addition, the trailer may also contain a unique identifier for the file, and must contain the end of file marker.[5] The entire trailer may not actually be located at the end of the file, depending on how the file was generated. In some cases, the trailer entry at the end of the file simply points to another trailer location by byte offset. For instance, the trailer at the end of a sample linearized

Figure 5 Trailer

file is shown in Figure 5. In this example, there were 6 cross-reference entries. This trailer entry points to additional trailer data at byte offset 116 in the file.

4 PDF Risk Areas

This analysis identifies eleven main types of hidden data, metadata, and embedded content that may be found in PDF files. These areas constitute the most common areas that will affect users who want to share PDF files with other parties. These areas form the basis for the sanitization procedure that is outlined in Section 5. As each risk area is reviewed, the mitigation step will be briefly presented so that the applicability of the sanitization process to reducing the threat can be identified. The areas are organized from the simplest to the most complex.

4.1 Metadata

Metadata is a common occurrence in PDF files because the data that is contained in the document is typically populated automatically by the PDF conversion application. In addition, while Acrobat Professional offers an interface to manipulate this data, the free Acrobat reader only allows the user to view the data. The fields are user accessible in many versions of Acrobat Professional by going to 'File' and selecting 'Properties' as shown in Figure 6. Most metadata can be manually removed through this interface, such as the creator, title, author, and producing application. Other fields such as modified date, created date, and document and instance ID's are not as easy to remove through the application. The ID's help to identify when multiple different documents are versions of the same source document, and are generally not sensitive unless the author does not want viewers to be able to tell that the files came from the same source document.

Acrobat Professional also provides an advanced interface that can be reached from the basic properties window by selecting the 'Additional Metadata' button and then selecting the 'Advanced' option in the window that appears. This interface displays the document information dictionary metadata and XMP metadata stored in the document. The advanced interface is shown in Figure 7. They are grouped according to the schema that defines their structure. From this menu, the user has the option of deleting each category of metadata individually.

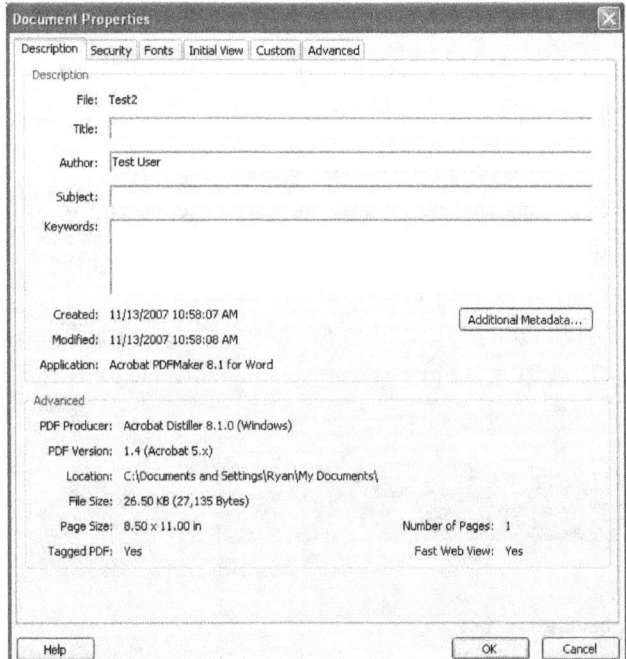

Figure 6 Basic Document Properties Interface

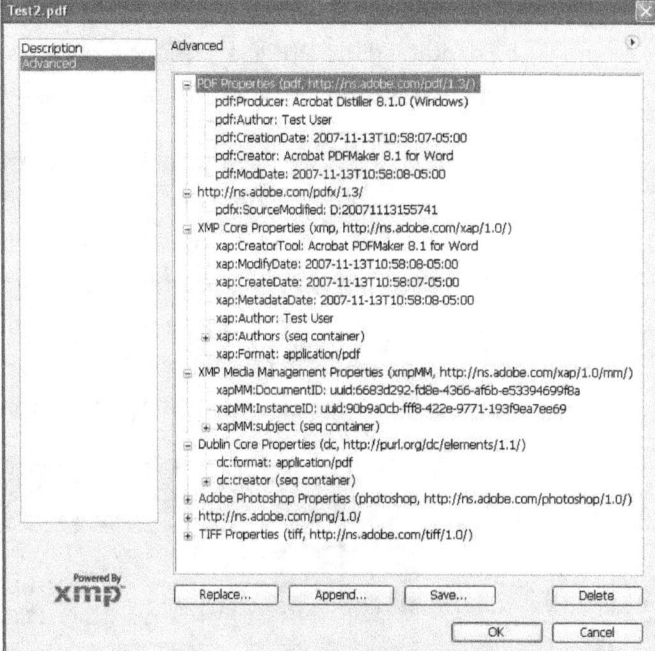

Figure 7 Advanced Document Properties Interface

XMP is powerful and can potentially include metadata that originated from other applications. For instance, an image that contained camera metadata that was edited in Photoshop before being inserted into the PDF may have its own XMP entry. [6] The XMP Specification available on Adobe's site provides more specific details about what XMP is, how the structures are defined, and how XMP may be embedded in different application files. [7]

4.2 Embedded Content and Attached Files

PDF files may contain a significant variety of different content types. These may either be embedded or attached. Embedded content generally appears and runs as part of a page in the file, even though third party applications might provide the functionality necessary to support the content. Attached files generally require that users open the file with an external application, and are not displayed as part of the PDF file.

A variety of different embedded content types may be present in a PDF file. The newer versions of PDF support multimedia such as Flash, Windows Media Video, and QuickTime content. Each of these content types may contain hidden data or metadata that can be difficult to review. In addition, the way that content is stored and encoded may make it difficult to accurately and thoroughly examine the contents.

Acrobat also supports multimedia that combines with other features, such as audio comments for reviewing. Alternatively, audio may be directly embedded in the file. When audio (or other multimedia) exists in a PDF file, the author has the option of changing the poster (icon) that represents the object. If a plain white image is chosen without a border, the content may be invisible within the file. The variability in how multimedia content may be displayed increases the chance that such content might be contained in a PDF file without the publisher's knowledge. PDF also supports other embedded content such as PostScript, which cannot be opened within the Acrobat interface.

In Adobe Acrobat, file attachments are displayed in a dedicated interface area. In some older versions of the Acrobat Reader, the file attachments interface was not visible to users. Only the full Acrobat application could access these objects. Attachments are now shown in the current versions (8) of both the reader and authoring tool. The reader allows the user to open, save, and search attached files. The full version of Acrobat also supports adding and deleting attachments. An example of the file attachment interface for Acrobat Professional 8 is shown in Figure 8. In this example, a Word File, a text file, and a PDF file have been attached to the PDF document.

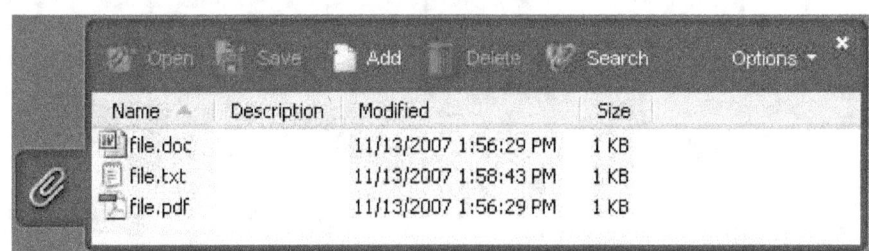

Figure 8 Acrobat Professional Attachments Interface

Attachments and embeddings may exist in a PDF file for a variety of reasons, but their presence presents potentially significant hidden data risks. For these reasons, the sanitization process outlined in this document recommends removing all embeddings and attachments before the file can be safely distributed.

4.3 Scripts

As with most other complex document formats, the benefits and risks of scripts are significant. By default, the Acrobat Reader enables active content such as JavaScript. Such scripts can be configured to load when the document is opened. A user can turn this functionality off, but most users do not disable scripts because there are legitimate uses for them. One example of a legitimate script feature is being able to detect the reader version to ensure that it at least matches the version of the document. If the user does not have the required version, they can be directed to Adobe's site to download an updated reader.

While scripts may enrich the document consumer's experience on an internal network, they also may contain more information than the author intends to publish. Examples of types of information that may be inadvertently released include system data, network attributes, and business process data.

Acrobat offers a simple JavaScript Editor as well as a JavaScript debugger. Both are available in the 'Advanced' menu in the 'Document Processing' area as shown in Figure 9. Document actions can be tied to scripts, so that code can be executed when the file is closed, printed, or saved.

Adobe has an extensive guide that shows developers how to use JavaScript within a PDF file.[8] Some of the other uses for JavaScript include manipulating or transmitting sensitive form data, reading or editing metadata, reviewing, layering control, and many other examples. The sanitization steps in this document include removing all JavaScript from PDF files. This will have impacts for some functionality that users might prefer to keep.

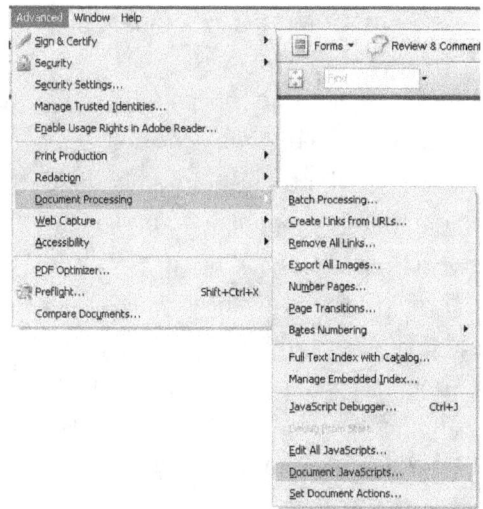

Figure 9 Document JavaScripts Menu

4.4 Hidden Layers

The ability to use layers enables file authors to include multiple representations of content within a single viewable area. This is commonly used in architectural and engineering designs. It would enable a user, for instance, to view different components of a complex object in the same context by changing the visibility of the component parts. In many cases, this might also be tied to JavaScript to control layer visibility. A button could be presented to the user to allow them to control which individual components are displayed.

Layers may be created automatically by Acrobat extensions within external applications such as AutoCAD and Visio. Whether the layers are maintained during PDF conversion depends upon the source object's properties and the conversion settings. When properly configured, the layers are maintained in the resulting PDF file following conversion and can be accessed through the 'Layers' interface as shown in Figure 10. This can be accessed by selecting the 'View' menu, selecting 'Navigation Panels', then ensuring that 'Layers' is checked.

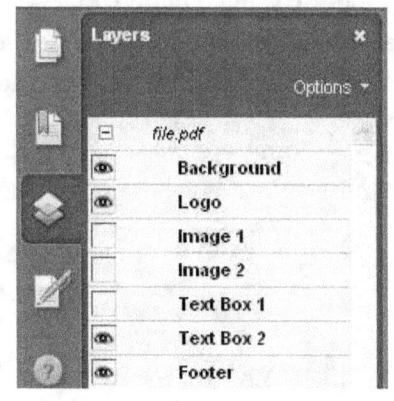

Figure 10 Acrobat Layers Interface

Layers may be difficult to effectively evaluate. In addition, non-visible layers may contain malicious content or embeddings that the user might not want to retain. For these reasons, the sanitization procedures outlined in this document recommend flattening layers so that all data is displayed in a single layer. Another recommended sanitization procedure in this document, the removal of scripts and embeddings, further necessitates the removal of layers because this action will prevent viewers from being able to effectively navigate layered content if scripts were tied to the layer navigation features.

4.5 Embedded Search Index

For large documents, text searches can be time consuming for users. PDF provides an embedded search index capability to make text searches faster. This is accessed through the 'Advanced' menu, in the 'Document Processing' submenu, by selecting 'Manage Embedded Index'. The index interface appears as shown in Figure 11.

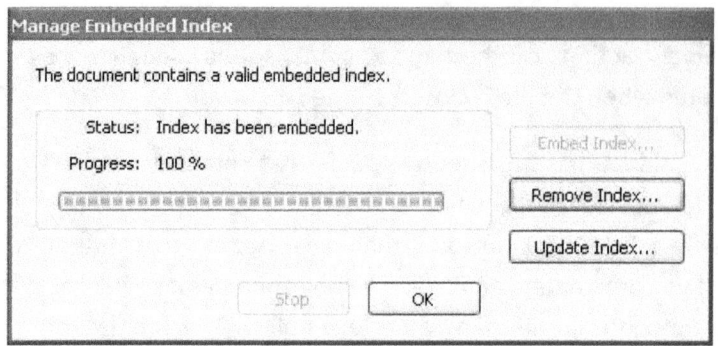

Figure 11 Embedded Search Index Interface

An embedded search index helps make user searches faster, and is especially useful in very large documents. However, a search index may retain content from previous versions of a document that has been removed. For this reason, it is imperative that embedded search indexes are removed prior to distribution.

4.6 Stored Interactive Form Data

PDF form features are increasingly common, and are being used to collect user data that would otherwise have been written or typed into traditional forms. Acrobat even enables form authors to include a submit button that sends forms completed by users to a pre-established email address. JavaScript could alternatively be used to enable custom form functionality, automatically fill some fields, or to facilitate complex data interaction with external sources.

Forms are typically created within the Acrobat interface, but can also be created in combination with LiveCycle Designer or from almost any source application if the fields are tagged correctly prior to conversion. The forms toolbar in Acrobat Professional is shown in Figure 12.

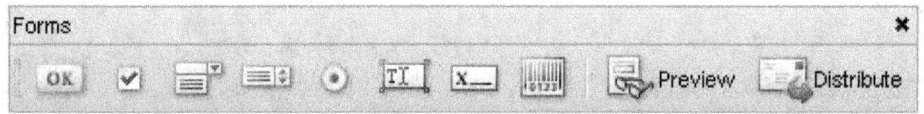

Figure 12 Acrobat Forms Menu

Similar to scripts, form fields, stored user data, and form processing information may contain information that is not intended for release beyond organizational boundaries. In addition, communication mechanisms used to transmit this data could create additional hidden data risks. For these reasons, the recommended sanitization approach outlined in this document recommends flattening all form fields (as well as removing any connections or scripts associated with the forms). This maintains the appearance of the file while significantly reducing the risks associated with forms.

4.7 Reviewing and Commenting

Collaborative features are commonly used for group communication about the content of a document. When multiple users seek to work collaboratively, the ability to work with a single medium to share ideas is critical. For this reason, commenting and reviewing features are commonly used during the creation of documents. Yet, when the document is ready to be distributed, these features may still retain data not intended to be shared with the target audience.

Acrobat offers a variety of reviewing features. The menu is shown in Figure 13. The tools allow a reviewer to mark text for change, to comment on specific items, and even to incorporate multimedia into the file to help users share ideas. The problem is that once all the collective ideas have been incorporated, the reviewing features generally need to be removed. Comments may reveal Intellectual Property Information, personal opinions that do not reflect the position of the organization as a whole, or at the very least may contain content not approved by the appropriate release authorities for sharing.

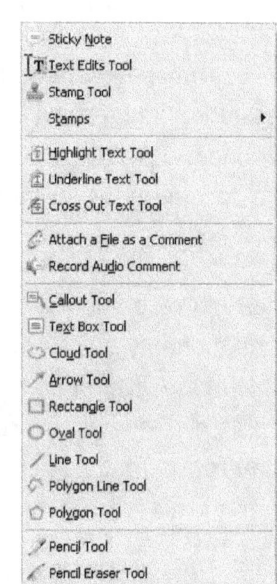

For these reasons, the sanitization recommendations in this document include the removal of all reviewing and commenting data. Removing this content will significantly reduce the hidden data risk in many cases.

Figure 13 Acrobat Reviewing Menu

4.8 Hidden Page, Image, and Update Data

PDF files may be generated in several ways. They can be created in a single pass, where the content is created from the beginning to the end. They can be linearized, where the content is organized in a way that makes the information necessary to load the beginning of the file available first for fast web loading. Or, PDF files can be incrementally updated. Incremental updates occur when an existing PDF file is modified without regenerating all of the content.

When PDF files are updated incrementally, the previous versions of data in the file may still be retained, but it is not visible to the user. This poses a potentially significant risk. PDF's created in a single pass may not be organized in the most efficient way. For these reasons, the recommended sanitization approach includes regenerating the file using the PDF optimization procedure provided by Adobe Acrobat 8. By doing this, inefficiencies and hidden data risks related to single pass or incrementally updated files can be removed.

4.9 Obscured Text and Images

Text can be obscured in a number of different ways. For instance, white text on a white background (or other text of any color matching the background color) could be hidden, but still be extractable if all the contents are copied and pasted into notepad. The same technique can also extract text that is inadvertently hidden behind images. This can be a tricky issue in document management, because objects copied and pasted from one program into another prior to the PDF conversion process could contain text that is not easy to detect.

Images have a similar risk because they may be hidden behind other images. In addition, high resolution images can be displayed in a small footprint, so significant image data may be unnecessarily retained. When this occurs, more information may be stored in the file than the user can see. When the document is subsequently shared, sensitive data may be released.

The image downsampling that is part of the recommended sanitization process helps to address the high resolution issue, but overlapped images continue to pose a problem. One reason that they cannot simply be removed is that it may be difficult to tell whether the images have transparency, in which case overlapping could be a legitimate and necessary state. Ideally, multiple images could be grouped so that non-visible portions could be discarded without negatively impacting transparent or semitransparent objects, but there does not currently appear to be any mechanism in Acrobat to support this.

Downsampling images helps solve the high resolution image issue. Overlapped images and obscured text are a more difficult challenge. Acrobat's 'Examine Document' utility offers a feature that facilitates the removal of text that is completely obscured by images or text that matches the background color. The tool also removes text that is similar to (but not exactly the same as) the background color and text that is only partially obscured by an object, within a pre-determined tolerance. Text that is outside of the tolerance limits, but still similar in color to the background or partially obscured will be retained. Images hidden by other images are also still retained. For these reasons, careful manual review should ideally be performed prior to document conversion to help ensure that obscured text and images are not inadvertently retained within a PDF file.

The addition of the examine document utility in this process is intended to address the obscured text issue when the text is completely obscured by an object or when it exactly matches the background color. However, there is residual risk in this area that must be recognized.

4.10 PDF (Non-Displayed) Comments

In the PDF format, comments may be inserted into the binary data that are not displayed by Acrobat. They can be used to provide supplemental information about how components of the file are structured or information about where the data was generated. Comments appear in the binary of the file preceded by the percent sign (%). Because these comments are not displayed within Acrobat, they can contain data that is difficult to review.

The potential hidden data threat necessitates the removal of comments from the binary content of the file. The recommended sanitization procedure in this document involves regenerating the PDF content in Acrobat, at which time comments are discarded. This reduces the associated threat, but also may inhibit the ability to interoperate with other applications in the unlikely event that they use and depend on these comments.

4.11 Unreferenced Data

Data contained in a PDF document may be unreferenced. For instance, an object might exist in the body of a PDF file that is not referenced by the cross-reference table. In this case, that content will be hidden and generally does not appear in the Acrobat application. There are few limitations on what can exist between objects in a PDF file, so almost anything could be stored there. This creates a significant hidden data risk. The sanitization procedure outlined in this document involves regenerating the PDF file. When this is done, any unreferenced objects should be discarded. This reduces the chance that hidden content could be unintentionally released that contains sensitive data.

5 Removing Risk Area Content

Adobe Acrobat Professional 8.1 offers multiple tools to help remove hidden data and metadata. The 'PDF Optimizer' and 'Examine Document' tools both allow users to take a PDF document and remove sensitive data. The PDF optimization process has the added benefit of generally making the file smaller and ensuring that it is structured in the most efficient manner for common viewing scenarios such as inside a web browser over the Internet.

The relative robustness of Acrobat to errors or malformed content, especially compared to open source or custom tools, is a primary consideration in the recommendation that the integrated toolsets be leveraged. The PDF optimization process regenerates the content and helps ensure that the result is well formed, does not contain undesired hidden content, and is as efficient as possible.

The sanitization process includes five steps. The first step is preparatory and involves minimizing the presence of hidden data, metadata, and embedded content in the source file prior to converting to PDF (if possible). The second step is to configure the security settings of Acrobat to minimize any risks associated with opening the file for sanitization. The third step is to run the 'Preflight' utility. This ensures that the file can be successfully converted to the target format, which is a PDF version 7 file. The fourth step is to run the PDF Optimizer utility. This regenerates the PDF content and strips out hidden data, metadata, and embedded content as well as file attachments. The fifth step is to run the 'Examine Document' utility to identify and remove any residual hidden data, especially hidden text.

5.1 Detailed Sanitization Procedure

Step 1: Sanitize Source File

Source applications have varying levels of complexity, but most file types have some potential for containing content that should not be retained for static publication. If the application that generated the source file has a sanitization utility, it should be applied before converting to PDF.

Step 2: Configure Security Settings

Prior to opening a document for sanitization, three security configuration settings must be configured. The first setting is to ensure that all applicable Acrobat updates have been downloaded and installed. The second is to disable JavaScript. To change or verify this setting, select the 'Edit' menu from the top menu bar and then select the 'Preferences' option. Then select the 'JavaScript' category, and uncheck the 'Enable Acrobat JavaScript' box as shown in Figure 14. Click the 'OK' button so that the change takes effect.

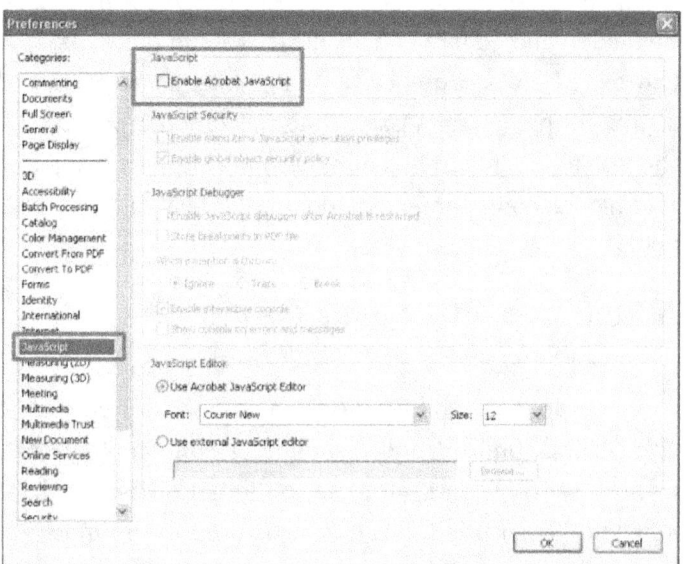

Figure 14 Acrobat JavaScript Settings

The third configuration procedure is to verify that the trust manager settings are set appropriately. Acrobat provides a preset execution list of allowed and disallowed file types. This is a fairly extensive list, and the settings may be changed if a user has attempted to open one of these file types and checked the box to always allow the content type. To reset the lists to the defaults, go to the 'Edit' menu, select 'Preferences', and select the 'Trust Manager' option. In the window that appears (shown in Figure 15), select the

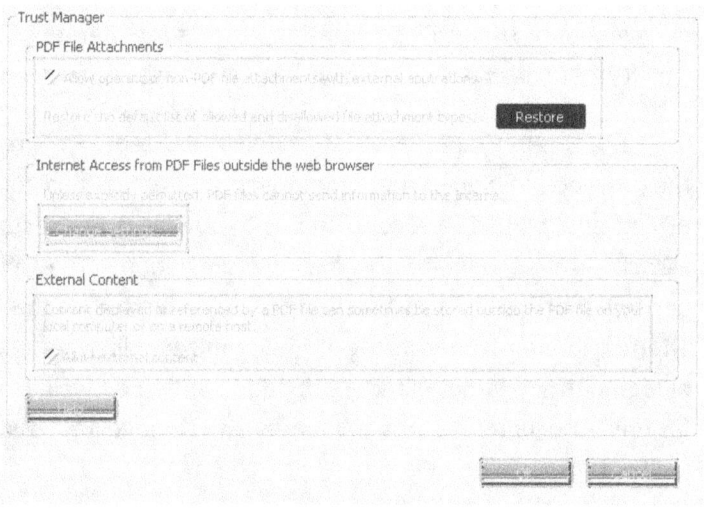

Figure 15 Acrobat Trust Manager Menu

'Restore' button and click 'OK' when prompted. If the button is grayed out, then no changes to the default have been made and no further action needs to be taken for these lists. Alternatively, the 'Allow opening of non-PDF file attachments with external applications' can be unchecked to prevent all attachments from being able to be opened, although this may impact the user of the application if they frequently work with PDF's that contain legitimate attachments.

Verify that PDF files prompt before accessing Internet content by choosing the "Change Settings" button. In the menu that appears, choose "Let me specify a list of allowed and blocked web sites" and ensure that the default behavior is set to 'Always ask'. Alternatively, 'Block all web sites' could be chosen, but this will prevent all hyperlinks from functioning in PDF files, which may impede desired functionality. Finally, verify that the 'Allow external content' is unchecked to ensure that the file does not reference data outside of the file container.

Note: Additional information about these and other Acrobat security settings is available on Adobe's website.[9]

Step 3: Run Preflight

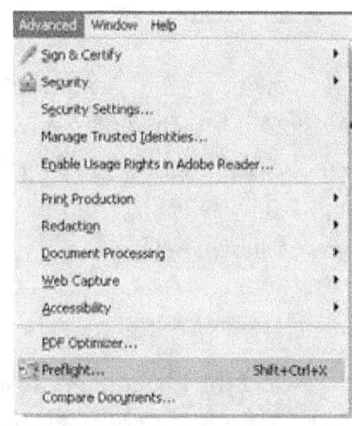

Open the file ('filename.pdf') in Adobe Acrobat Professional 8.1 or higher. Select the 'Advanced' menu as shown in Figure 16, and choose the 'Preflight' option.

Figure 16 'Advanced' Menu

Preflight ensures that the file contents are compatible with the destination version, and applies 'fixups' as necessary. In the menu that appears, select 'Compatible with Acrobat 7' as shown in Figure 17. Ensure that 'Run Preflight profile without applying fixups' is unchecked. Click the 'Execute' button.

A warning dialog box may appear that states 'This Preflight profile contains fixups that may permanently change the file'. Click 'OK' to continue.

You may be prompted to save the file. If so, save the file with a different name (such as 'filename2.pdf') and continue.

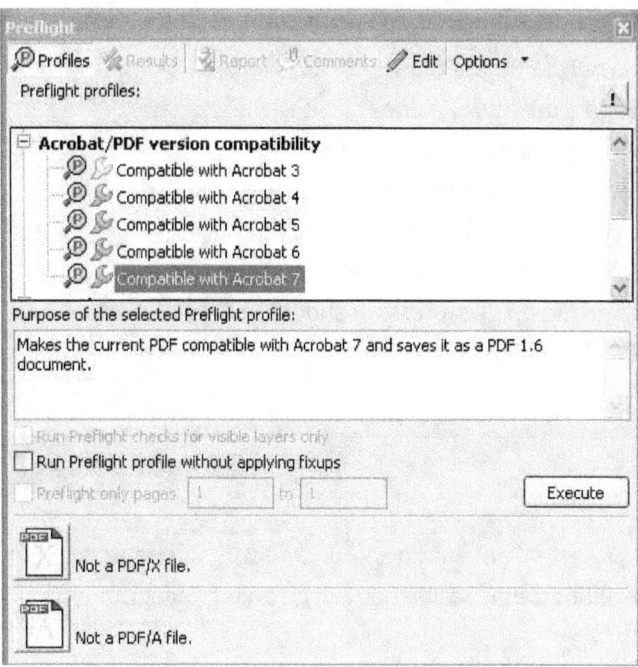

Figure 17 Preflight Profiles Window

A summary of the Preflight results is presented as shown in Figure 18. Carefully review any warnings.

Note: If an error is encountered, this may prevent the rest of the sanitization process from completing normally. Attempt to regenerate the PDF from the source application, if possible, and then reattempt to complete the sanitization process.

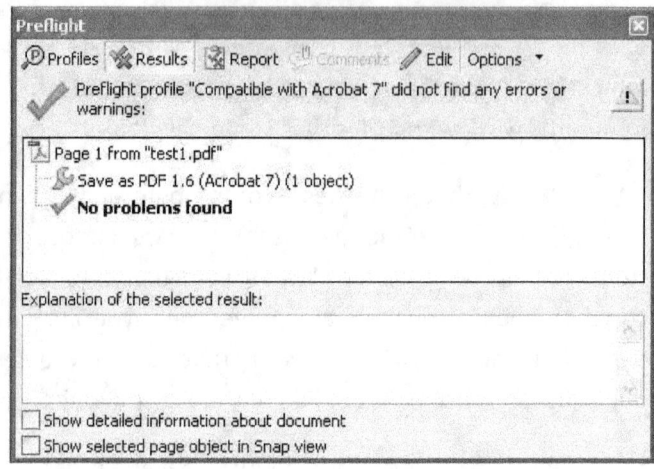

Figure 18 Preflight Results Window

Step 4: Run the PDF Optimizer

Now open the 'Advanced' menu again and choose the 'PDF Optimizer' option. If the PDF file contains other attached files, a warning message appears. Click 'OK' to continue. The attached files will be removed during PDF optimization. The PDF Optimizer window appears. Change the version to Acrobat 7.0 by selecting 'Acrobat 7.0 and later', in the 'Make compatible with' area near the top of the window as shown in Figure 19.

Select the Images Setting as shown in Figure 19. Choose Bicubic Downsampling to 150 pixels/inch for images above 225 pixels/inch. Compression should be 'JPEG' with 'High' quality. Repeat with the same settings for Grayscale Images. For monochrome images, choose Bicubic Downsampling to 300 pixels/inch for images above 450 pixels/inch. Compression should be 'CCITT Group 4'.

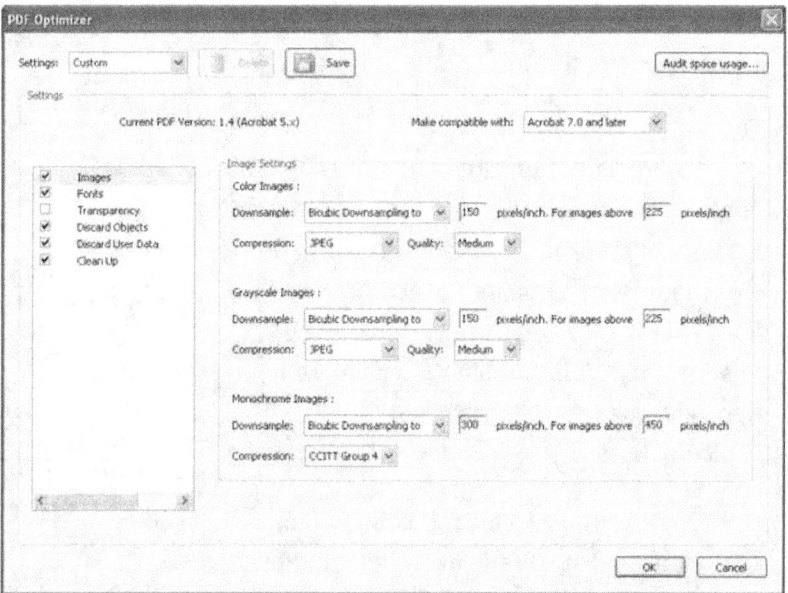

Figure 19 'Images' Setting in the 'PDF Optimizer' Window

If 'Fonts' is checked, it may be unchecked. Retaining the embedded fonts improves the likelihood that recipients will be able to accurately view the content, though size will be increased.

Optionally, the embedded fonts can be removed if only common fonts are used, but recipients may have trouble viewing the content in some cases. Transparency may also be unchecked.

Select the 'Discard Objects' setting. Check all available options as shown in Figure 20. Optionally, bookmarks may be retained by un-checking 'Discard bookmarks'. If bookmarks are retained, they should be manually reviewed using the bookmarks menu (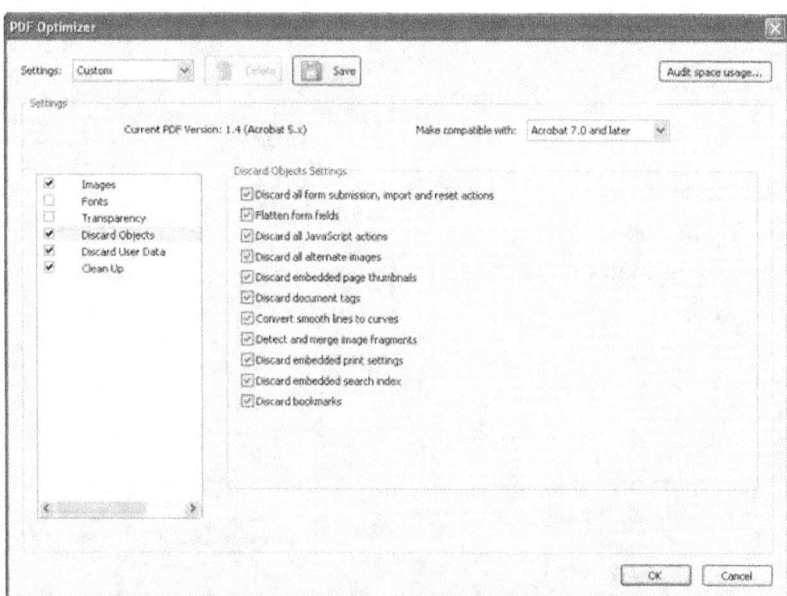) in the left navigation panel of Acrobat.

Figure 20 Discard Objects Option within the PDF Optimizer

Note: Document tags pose a hidden data risk. This procedure (specifically the checked option in Figure 18 for 'Discard document tags') removes them from the sanitized PDF. However, these tags can also provide enhanced accessibility for visually impaired users by describing the content so that assistive devices such as screen readers can provide contextual information. Tags also enable reflow for portability across varying device types so that content can be viewed on devices such as PDA's in a usable way. There are two options when accessibility and portability must be maintained.

1. (Recommended) Remove all tags during the sanitization, and then regenerate them from the sanitized document using Acrobat Professional according to the procedure outlined in Adobe's accessibility guide.[10] To do so, open the sanitized document in Acrobat Professional, select the 'Advanced' menu, then the 'Accessibility' option, and select 'Add Tags to Document'. This will likely provide a lower level of accessibility and portability than the source-generated tags provided, but offers the least likelihood that sensitive data is retained.

2. Retain the document tags and manually inspect the contents. This can be cumbersome if many tags exist. The biggest benefit from retaining the tags comes when the original PDF was generated from the source with the tagging option turned on and the source document was designed for accessibility (i.e. contains alt tags, has logical order, etc.). In Microsoft Office, the Acrobat plug-in checkbox for this setting is 'Enable accessibility and reflow with tagged PDF'. If that box was not initially checked when the PDF was created, retaining any tags in the PDF file may not provide significant value.
   Analysis Procedure: To manually review the tags, open the document in Acrobat Professional and opening the 'View' menu, selecting 'Navigation Panels', and then 'Tags'.

More information about Acrobat accessibility and Section 508 is available on Adobe's website.[11]

Select the 'Discard User Data' setting as shown in Figure 21. Make sure that all options are checked.

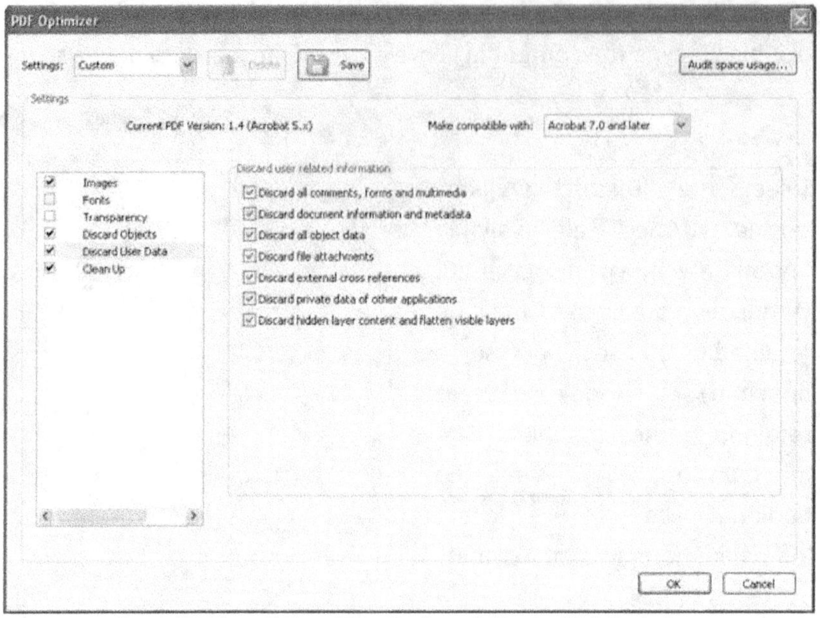

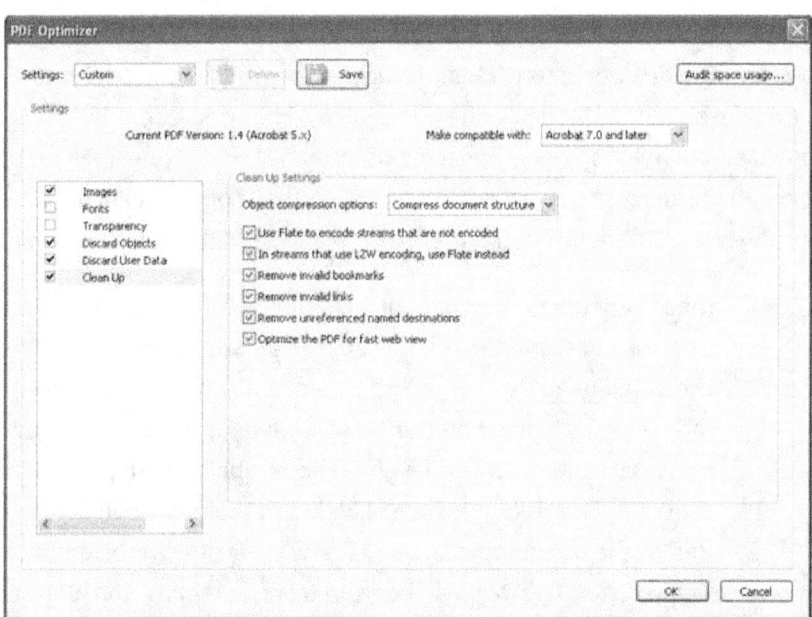

Figure 21 Discard User Data Option within the PDF Optimizer

Select the 'Clean Up' setting as shown in Figure 22. Make sure that in the Object Compression Options, 'Compress document structure' is selected. All other options in this settings window should also be selected.

Figure 22 Clean Up Option within the PDF Optimizer

Once you have finished configuring the optimizer, click 'OK' to continue. Acrobat will prompt you to save the optimized file. Save this file with a different name (such as 'filename3.pdf'), and leave it open within Acrobat.

Note: If the file is password protected, you will need to provide the password to continue.
Note: If you encounter a stream-related error message, the original file may be corrupt (although this should be rare if Preflight completed without error). Try regenerating the file with the original source

application and Adobe Acrobat Professional, then repeat the optimization process. Any error messages encountered indicate that the file may not have been sanitized successfully, and you should not continue because the risk areas may remain in the files.

The preceding 'PDF Optimizer' steps can also be saved in a settings profile for easier configuration on subsequent document sanitizations. To do so, ensure that all of the settings in the 'PDF Optimizer' match the recommendations in this document. Then click the 'Save' button at the top of the 'PDF Optimizer' window. You will be prompted for a name for this configuration. Choose something descriptive such as 'NSA Sanitization'. Now click 'OK'. The configuration has been saved and will be available the next time you perform a sanitization.

Step 5: Run the Examine Document Utility

The final step is to run the document examination utility. This helps to find text hidden behind objects as well as any other areas that might have been missed in the previous steps. Select 'Document' menu, and then select the 'Examine Document' option. The menu appears as shown in Figure 23. If any boxes are grayed out, those hidden data areas were not found and the box is inactive. All of the active boxes (except bookmarks if you want to retain them) should be checked.

Note: 'Deleted hidden page and image content' may appear, even if this data does not exist in the document. There is no reason to be concerned if this item appears even after you finish the sanitization.

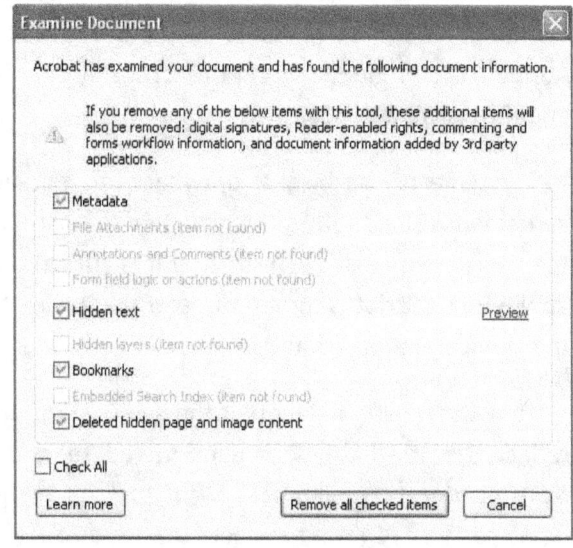

Figure 23 Acrobat 'Examine Document' menu

Press the 'Remove all checked items' button at the bottom of the menu. A confirmation is displayed as shown in Figure 24. Save the file (you should choose a descriptive name now such as 'filename_sanitized.pdf' that clearly distinguishes this version from previous un-sanitized versions). The document is now ready to be shared.

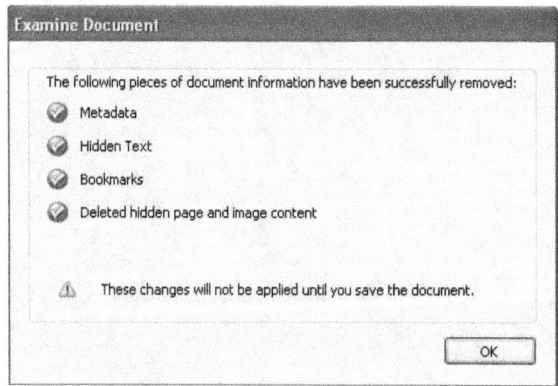

Figure 24 'Examine Document' Results Window

6 Conclusion

PDF files offer several benefits over other file types. They enable the appearance of the content to be maintained across varying client types, can be read by the widely available Acrobat reader, and have less hidden data and malicious content risk than some other file types. At the same time, the malicious content and hidden data risks that do exist related to the PDF file type need to be carefully managed through a sanitization procedure such as the one outlined here. The use of Adobe Acrobat Professional to sanitize PDF files has several benefits and drawbacks.

One of the key benefits is that Adobe has significant knowledge about the inner workings of PDF, so their tools are among the most robust available. By using a sophisticated PDF utility, the sanitized file can be simultaneously optimized for smaller size, faster loading, and ensure well-formed content that will be readable by the broadest possible target audience. As new features are added, Adobe will continue to be on the forefront of compatibility because they develop both the specification and the Acrobat toolset.

One of the biggest drawbacks to this approach is that if malformed or malicious content is contained within the file, opening it within Acrobat for performing the sanitization process could expose the user to some risk. This is why it is critical that the user ensures that the latest updates have been applied, JavaScript is turned off, and the Acrobat security settings are configured in a way that reduces the chance that malicious content can harm their system.

Users who implement the sanitization procedures described in this document will significantly reduce the risk that hidden data, metadata, and embedded content are contained in the sanitized file. No procedure can eliminate all of the risk associated with publishing data using complex document types such as PDF that support the inclusion of a wide range of data types. However, the informed handling of these document types will reduce the associated risks and allow users to exchange data in a format that is generally accepted and widely used.

References

[1] Adobe's web site. *Adobe*
http://www.adobe.com

[2] Adobe Acrobat and industry standards. *Adobe*
http://www.adobe.com/products/acrobat/standards.html

[3] Redacting with Confidence: How to Safely Publish Sanitized Reports Converted from Word to PDF. *NSA*
http://www.nsa.gov/snac/vtechrep/I333-TR-015R-2005.PDF

[4] PDF Reference 1.7. p. 95 *Adobe*
http://www.adobe.com/devnet/pdf/pdf_reference.html

[5] PDF Reference 1.7. p. 96-7 *Adobe*
http://www.adobe.com/devnet/pdf/pdf_reference.html

[6] Adobe XMP for Creative Professionals. *Adobe*
http://www.adobe.com/products/xmp/pdfs/xmp_creativepros.pdf

[7] XMP Specification. *Adobe*
http://www.adobe.com/devnet/xmp/pdfs/xmp_specification.pdf

[8] Acrobat JavaScript Scripting Guide. *Adobe*
http://partners.adobe.com/public/developer/en/acrobat/sdk/pdf/javascript/AcroJSGuide.pdf

[9] Document Security User Guide. *Adobe*
http://www.adobe.com/devnet/acrobat/pdfs/doc_security_user_guide.pdf

[10] Creating Accessible Documents with Adobe Acrobat 7.0. *Adobe*
http://www.adobe.com/enterprise/accessibility/pdfs/acro7_pg_ue.pdf

[11] Adobe Accessibility Resource Center
http://www.adobe.com/accessibility

www.ingramcontent.com/pod-product-compliance
Lightning Source LLC
Chambersburg PA
CBHW08080429O526
45790CB00008B/3584